YOU ARE GOING

and

THIS IS NOT CULTURALLY SIGNIFICANT

Adam Scott-Rowley

T0253038

methuen | drama

LONDON • NEW YORK • OXFORD • NEW DELHI • SYDNEY

METHUEN DRAMA
Bloomsbury Publishing Plc
50 Bedford Square, London, WC1B 3DP, UK
1385 Broadway, New York, NY 10018, USA
29 Earlsfort Terrace, Dublin 2, Ireland

BLOOMSBURY, METHUEN DRAMA and the Methuen
Drama logo are trademarks of Bloomsbury Publishing Plc

First published in Great Britain 2024

A catalogue record for this book is available from the British Library.

Library of Congress Control Number: 2024935387

ISBN: PB: 978-1-3505-1267-2
ePDF: 978-1-3505-1268-9
eBook: 978-1-3505-1269-6

Series: Modern Plays

Typeset by Mark Heslington Ltd, Scarborough, North Yorkshire

To find out more about our authors and books visit
www.bloomsbury.com and sign up for our newsletters.

YOU ARE GOING TO DIE

by Adam Scott-Rowley
with Joseph Prowen & Tom Morley

THIS IS NOT CULTURALLY SIGNIFICANT

by Adam Scott-Rowley
Dramaturgy by Joseph Prowen

THE PRODUCTION EXCHANGE
presents

YOU ARE GOING TO DIE

★ ★ ★ ★ ★ *"Takes you places you'd never dream of or dare to step into of your own volition."* – The Theatre Times

★ ★ ★ ★ ★ *"The most fascinating, defiant, mind-tingling performance artist you'll ever see."* – Everything Theatre

★ ★ ★ ★ *"Physically astonishing and vocally brilliant 60 minutes hovers between tragedy and farce, dread and hilarity"* Lyn Gardner for The Stage

Created and performed by Adam Scott-Rowley
Co-created with Joseph Prowen and Tom Morley
Lighting Design by Matt Cater
Finale Song Composition by Phil McDonnell
Finale Song Mastered by Dominic Brennan
Sound Design by Sam Baxter
Production Photography by Ryan Buchanan
Marketing Consultant Sam McAuley
PR Consultant Clióna Roberts, CRPR

Thursday 18 April to Saturday 4 May 2024 at The Large, Southwark Playhouse Borough

For The Production Exchange

Artistic Director Colin Blumenau
Producer Penelope Saward

www.theproductionexchange.com

YOU ARE GOING TO DIE was first produced by Adam Scott-Rowley at VAULT Festival London 2023, then subsequently at Summerhall for the Edinburgh Festival 2023, and Teater Katapult Aarhus, Denmark 2023.

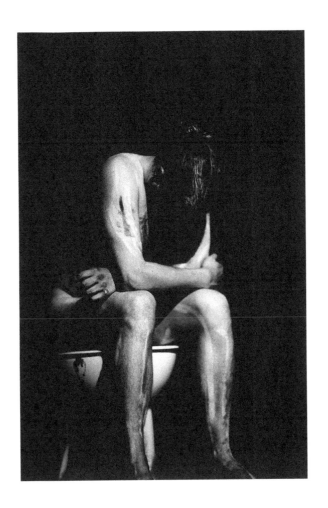

Adam Scott-Rowley
presents

THIS IS NOT CULTURALLY SIGNIFICANT

✶ ✶ ✶ ✶ ✶ *"Deeply sad in parts, this performance is a 55 minute scream for help, and it sounds beautiful."* – Independent

Created and performed by Adam Scott-Rowley
Dramaturgy by Joseph Prowen
Original Lighting Concept by Will Scarnell
Lighting Design by Matt Cater
Sound Design by Graeme Pugh
Production Photography by Bessell McNamee

THIS IS NOT CULTURALLY SIGNIFICANT was first produced by Adam Scott-Rowley at the Etcetera Theatre London 2015, then subsequently at The Pleasance for the Edinburgh Festival 2016. The production was then co-produced with Jamie Eastlake for VAULT Festival London 2017, The Bunker Theatre London 2017, Gilded Balloon for the Edinburgh Festival 2017 and Teater Katapult Aarhus, Denmark 2017 and 2018.

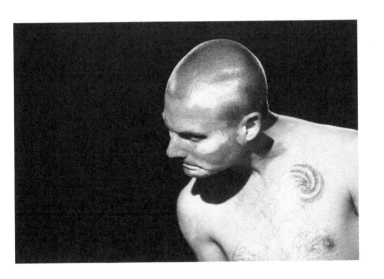

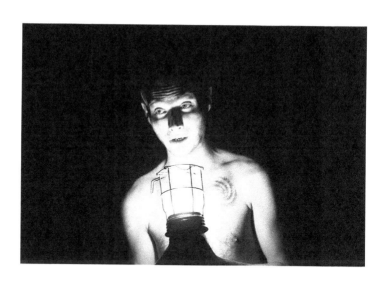

ADAM SCOTT-ROWLEY trained at the London Academy of Music and Dramatic Art (LAMDA). He is a multidisciplinary theatre practitioner covering acting, writing, directing and teaching.

Adam's creative focus is rooted in defying traditional theatrical norms, celebrating the avant-garde and kindling compassion in the most unlikely of places.

As a practitioner, Adam works at The Danish National School of Performing Arts where he teaches and directs his theatre and performance methodology 'The Sensitised Theatre'. He has also taught at the Copenhagen International School of Performing Arts, the Royal Central School of Speech and Drama, Mountview, ArtsEd, and the National Youth Theatre.

Adam is a qualified secular mindfulness practitioner and is authorised to teach mindfulness by the Mindfulness Association, having completed their Mindfulness, Compassion, Insight and two-year teacher training pathway. He holds a postgraduate degree in the Studies of Mindfulness from the University of Aberdeen.

Awards for Adam's performance in THIS IS NOT CULTURALLY SIGNIFICANT include: 2017 Offie Nomination for Best Male Performance; WINNER Stand-Out Performance at the Fringe 2017; WINNER Best Solo Performance at the Fringe 2017; and WINNER Show of the Week at VAULT Festival 2018.

Awards for Adam's performance in YOU ARE GOING TO DIE include: 2023 Offie Nomination for IDEA Production: Devised or Physical Theatre and 2023 VAULT Festival Nomination for the ORIGINS AWARD.

www.AdamScottRowley.com

JOSEPH PROWEN is an actor, musician, writer and director. He trained as an actor at the London Academy of Music and Dramatic Art (LAMDA).

Acting credits include: theatre: *A Christmas Carol, Twelfth Night* (Royal Shakespeare Company); *Piaf* (Nottingham Playhouse/Leeds Playhouse); *A Midsummer Night's Dream* (Scoot Theatre, tour); *Trial by Laughter* (Watermill and UK tour); *Bury the Hatchet, Boris III* (Vaults); *A View From Islington North* (Arts Theatre/Out of Joint); *Single Spies* (Chichester Festival Theatre/Birmingham Rep/UK tour);

Jefferson's Garden, Dick Whittington (Watford Palace Theatre); *Teddy* (Southwark Playhouse); *An Ideal Husband* (Chichester Festival Theatre).

Television: *Father Brown, Decline and Fall, And Then There Were None, Casualty* (BBC); *Midsomer Murders* (ITV).

Film: *Chevalier* (Searchlight Pictures).

www.josephprowen.com

TOM MORLEY has worked as an actor in a breadth of roles across television, film, and stage. His television appearances include *Gentleman Jack*, *Becoming Elizabeth*, *FBI International*, *Call the Midwife*, *Grantchester*, *Holby City*, *Humans*, *The Musketeers*, *Father Brown* and *Downton Abbey*. Film credits include *Red Sparrow*.

Theatre credits include *Owners*, *The Funeral Director*, *This Beautiful Future*, *A Room with a View*, *Five Finger Exercise*, *The Comedy of Errors*, *Pitcairn*.

www.tommorleyactor.com

MATT CATER. Following a childhood fascination with both science and theatre, Matt went on to train at the London Academy of Music and Dramatic Art (LAMDA) where he studied stage management and technical theatre, focusing on lighting design and production electrics.

Since graduating in 2014 he has amassed experience across a variety of entertainment lighting disciplines: designing for theatre, dance and opera; working internationally as a lighting technician and programmer; and has specialised in bespoke LED solutions for TV and live events. Bringing these influences together allows Matt to blend visual impact with subtle story telling.

Lighting Design credits include: *YOU ARE GOING TO DIE* (Edinburgh and VAULT Festival); *Iolanthe/Utopia Limited!/Pirates of Penzance* (Gilbert and Sullivan Festival, Buxton Opera House); *Tales of the Turntable* (ZooNation, Southbank Centre); *Cinderella/The Three Sisters/Beauty and The Beast/Gretel/Snow Queen* (Playbox); *HMS Pinafore* (ODL, Buxton Opera House); *The Rise and Fall of Little Voice* (Park Theatre); *L'incoranazione di Poppea* (Longborough Festival Opera); *Partenope/Candide* (Iford Arts Opera); *Un Ballo Un Maschera/Il Travatore* (Winslow Hall Opera); *YOU ARE GOING TO DIE* (VAULT

Festival); *La Belle Hélène* (New Sussex Opera); *Three Decembers* (ODL); *The Wreckers* (Arcadian Opera); *A Christmas Carol* (Windsor Castle); *People Who Need People* (VAULT Festival); *Beast on the Moon/Into the Numbers/The Busy World is Hushed* (Finborough Theatre); *Macbeth/Pericles* (LAMDA Sainsbury Theatre); *THIS IS NOT CULTURALLY SIGNIFICANT* (Edinburgh, The Bunker, VAULT Festival, Denmark); *One Last Thing (For Now)* (Old Red Lion); *Girl from Nowhere* (St James' Studio); *Verge of Strife* (Assembly Edinburgh); *Othello/Measure for Measure/The Island/Prince of Homburg/Mydidae/ Romeo and Juliet/Julius Caesar/Copenhagen/Boom/Lift Off* (LAMDA Linbury Studio); *As You Like It/Mary Shelley* (Pleasance Theatre, London).

www.mattcater.com

In 2023 **THE PRODUCTION EXCHANGE (TPE)** began its second decade. During its first decade it was busy delivering the organisation's charitable mission: to support early-career practitioners in the creative arts. Primarily a producer of theatre and a mentor of people at the start of their careers, the charity broadened its activities to become an artists' agency in 2015.

It has consolidated its work to provide a combination of development opportunities, professional management, mentoring services and pastoral support for early-career practitioners to empower them and help them to develop the necessary skills to become the next generation of creative artists.

The charity has an artistic policy whose priorities are to deliver a public-facing programme as producer, co-producer and/or general manager. The work is informed by the steadfast ambition to bring attention to authentic voices that are representative of disenfranchised communities of all kinds. The charity believes that these underheard voices are significant and relevant. They have a vital role to play in encouraging the Establishment to challenge the status quo. TPE works to create the circumstances and platforms from which they can be very clearly heard.

The Production Company specialises in new writing development and subsequent production.

Over the past decade TPE has produced and managed more than fifty projects of different sizes. From the first reading of a new play to the full production and touring of a number of works. The company believes that there is no substitute for learning on the job and it is always excited to help in any way it can – encouraging anyone who wants to start the ball rolling, to make contact. A full list of productions can be found on the company's website.

The Agency looks after actors, writers, directors, musical directors and designers.

Clients' work spans every area of the industry from the smallest theatre above a pub to a big Hollywood studio. The philosophy is simple: to be represented by TPE you must be brilliant at what you do. The company's fundamental belief is that it needs to represent the widest cross section of the society in which it is situated. In order to be true to that belief, the aim is to develop a client base that reflects the world in which we live. As part of that push for truly authentic and legitimate representation, TPE has a specific focus in representing artists from the D/deaf and the LGBTQ+ communities.

www.theproductionexchange.com

The Production Exchange is a registered charity in England and Wales.

Charity No. 1158517

Preface

THIS IS NOT CULTURALLY SIGNIFICANT

My debut play, first performed in 2016, was born out of caricature improvisations and stream of consciousness diarrhoea. It's a rebellion against the over-intellectualised, text-driven naturalism that pervades British theatre. At its conception, it was an exploration pushed to its limits by my unfaltering collaborators – magic mushrooms, weed, booze and a bunch of idiot friends at drama school – as we navigated the extremities of human expression against the backdrop of house parties, and ridiculous games such as 'who can do the most realistic impression of someone laughing, crying and cumming at the same time'.

I left drama school, miraculously relatively unscathed, with all of these wonderfully absurd and grotesque caricatures lurking in my mind, however, that is where they were to stay for a few years... until Brexit.

2016 came round and the UK was in a fucking mess. I needed a way to express my rage and despair, and fortunately, the caricatures obliged. The play premiered at the Etcetera Theatre followed by the Pleasance for the Edinburgh Festival. This early outing was actually performed fully clothed, and I was quick to notice that the audience would pull away from the caricatures and the heavy themes of the play, seemingly feeling that it was all just too intense and violent. Something had to be done to instil some vulnerability. I decided to perform it nude at VAULT Festival a year later, and it became a completely different beast. The shared vulnerability and connection with the audience was like nothing I had experienced before, as an actor or audience member, and so I stuck with it, and this formed one of the foundational principles of my methodology today.

Reflecting on the piece now for its publication has been a strange exercise, and I wondered how it would hold up to the last eight years. It saddens me to admit that its impact is as pronounced as ever. If anything, it has grown in relevance, depressingly mirroring the worsening degradation of the UK we find ourselves in in 2024.

THIS IS NOT CULTURALLY SIGNIFICANT is more about the overall experience than the sum of its parts. Allow the pain of the caricatures to shine through, and become a vessel for a much needed communal purge. Make it messy and perform it in a frenzy. We're all in this together.

YOU ARE GOING TO DIE

This play emerged from several places: a severe period of existential anxiety, the pandemic, a desire to make sense of my experiences in meditation, a need for connection, a wish to collaborate with friends, and an intention to culminate into a project the methodology I had been developing, 'The Sensitised Theatre', at Den Danske Scenekunstskole since 2018.

Unlike THIS IS NOT CULTURALLY SIGNIFICANT (TINCS), YOU ARE GOING TO DIE (YAGTD) is enveloped in an atmosphere of compassion rather than hatred, with my maturity reflecting a shift towards viewing human suffering through a lens of common humanity, drawing on ideas from Buddhist psychology. While there are some parallels with TINCS in its exploration of taking us to the very end of human expression, YAGTD significantly differs in its underlying tone. This shift towards compassion embraces our pain in a way that enables us to transcend a solitary, individualistic perspective and encourage a more collective, shared understanding of our suffering.

The play unfolds in a dream-like, meditative sequence, exploring themes around death, existentialism and the concept of the self – all ideas that have persistently haunted and intrigued me. At its core, YAGTD is a contemplation on the nature of human suffering and our impending annihilation, and the capacity for empathy, connection and compassion to overcome it. It invites us to see our collective anxieties, fears and frustrations, not as solitary challenges, but as elements of a broader interconnectedness that unites us in our search for meaning. With YAGTD, I aim to use the unique aspects of The Sensitised Theatre to cultivate a deeper, more empathetic connection among us all.

YAGTD is a collaboration between myself, Joseph Prowen, Tom Morley, Matt Cater and Phil McDonnell, without whom, it would be a very boring play indeed.

End Times

Writing at what feels like the twilight of British theatre, I've witnessed the industry's descent into mediocrity and despair under prolonged Tory governance. Theatres close, creativity wanes, and a once vibrant culture is now a pale imitation of its former self, engaged in a futile attempt to mimic the naturalistic escapism offered by TV and film. A short trip to Denmark or Germany confirms any suspicions that the British theatre industry is flogging a horse long dead, with our EU counterparts creating powerful and imaginative work, seemingly from some future century.

UK theatre today has become literal, patronising and devoid of the transformative power it once held. It has been reduced to a form of entertainment that fails to question, to confront, or to enlighten. Where is the theatre that truly wakes us up and forces us to face this pathetic complacency?

One could rail against the artistic directors for not taking enough risks, or the out-of-touch producers for commissioning work solely to line their own pockets, or indeed our directors for pitching rehashes of dusty old manuscripts from hundreds of years ago – but I am tentative to cast blame in this way. It ultimately comes down to money and subsidy, and the Tories being completely unwilling to value art beyond a commercial framing. The landscape has become so financially treacherous, that it is no wonder our art, deeply suffering, is void of risk.

And this of course perpetuates a vicious cycle; theatres don't want to take a risk with the fear of one poorly selling show resulting in financial ruin, and audiences becoming less enthusiastic about theatre generally because nobody is doing anything new. At some point something's got to give, and as an industry, we're going to have to become more courageous. I just hope that our artistic leaders and politicians cotton on to this sooner rather than later, or one can imagine a Britain in which Wetherspoons buys out every playhouse in the country.

The Sensitised Theatre

The Sensitised Theatre is my attempt to face this crisis. It is a call to abandon the stifling confines of PDFs and to embrace a process that prioritises emotional depth and physicality. This approach draws from the avant-garde[1] to challenge the status quo, aiming to connect on a level that precedes language, to engage the audience's emotions before their intellect kicks in.

---

[1] The term 'avant-garde' originated from the French military as an 'advanced guard', a unit that would scout ahead of the main force. In nineteenth-century French politics, it represented left-wing reformists pushing for radical societal changes. By mid-century, it also denoted a cultural movement, where art fused with politics to drive social transformation.

Contrary to perceptions of the avant-garde as elitist, practices in The Sensitised Theatre are ultimately down to earth and accessible in nature. This contrasts sharply with the current British theatre scene, often criticised for its endless overreliance on dialogue and cognition. The avant-garde, at its core, seeks a visceral connection, aiming to unearth and communicate the fundamentals of the human experience.

We must create theatre that asks the difficult questions and that instils empathy through the avant-garde rather than solely relying on text. This is about getting to the root of our shared human experience.

Creating a transformative theatre methodology requires a deep dive into both the performer's inner world and the collective consciousness of the audience. This methodology aims to forge a connection that transcends the conventional bounds of storytelling by using mindfulness, symbolism, queered narratives, the grotesque, existential philosophy, humour and nudity. The Sensitised Theatre serves as a desperately needed antidote to the inauthentic, riskless British theatre that we have, in recent times, so mindlessly accepted as the norm. Below are the key components of this approach:

Mindfulness and vulnerability

Mindfulness practices are foundational for actors to develop a consistent stage presence and vulnerability. Through techniques such as meditation, breathing exercises and body awareness, performers can anchor themselves in the present moment, enhancing their connection to their own emotions and to the audience. This presence allows for a genuine expression of vulnerability, breaking down barriers between the actor and the audience, and creating a shared emotional space.

Knocking down the fourth wall

The concept of liveness in theatre emphasises the unique, ephemeral nature of performance, where the audience's energy and reactions are integral to the shaping of the performance itself. Inspired by clowning and bouffon, this methodology encourages actors to remain open and responsive to the audience, allowing the collective experience and energy to guide the flow and intensity of the performance.

Symbolism

Beyond verbal language, this methodology leverages symbols and archetypal forms expressed through the actors' physicality to convey deeper meanings and universal truths. This approach draws on Grotowski and Artaud's work in physical expression, to tap into shared human experiences and emotions that resonate on a subconscious level. Through carefully crafted movements, gestures and emotional connection, performers can convey complex themes and tap into a system of expression that transcends words.

Queering linearity

Queering the narrative structure involves challenging traditional, linear storytelling methods and embracing non-linear, fragmented or alternative narrative forms. This approach seeks to disrupt normative 'straight' expectations and open up new ways of seeing and understanding the world. By queering the story, theatre can reflect the complexity and absurdity of human life, and challenge the audience to snap out of the familiarity and safety of being on auto-pilot.

Nudity

The use of nudity in performance is approached with the intention of expressing our shared humanity and the essence of pure experience, unmediated by social constructs or cognitive filters. Nudity is employed not for shock value but as a powerful symbol of vulnerability, authenticity and the universal human condition. It strips away some of the external markers of identity, class and culture, presenting the actor in their most raw and genuine form, creating a profound connection with the audience.

Humour

Humour is essential. If a play hasn't made you laugh or smile in the first five minutes, then honestly why bother sitting through the rest of it? Humour offers relief and perspective within the exploration of heavier themes. It serves as a powerful tool for resilience, allowing both performers and audience members to navigate through the extremities of human emotion and experience with lightness and silliness. It can bridge gaps, disarm resistance and open hearts. By weaving humour into our work, even the most profound or challenging subjects become approachable, encouraging a sense of shared humanity and mutual understanding.

The grotesque

The inclusion of the grotesque – through exaggerated, revolting, absurd or bizarre elements – challenges audiences to confront their preconceptions and discomforts, pushing the boundaries of conventional aesthetics. This use of the grotesque, whilst gratuitous, is a deliberate choice to explore the darker, hidden aspects of human nature and society. It serves to provoke thought, elicit strong emotional responses, and engage with the raw, ugly aspects of life. The grotesque can act as a mirror, reflecting the absurdities and contradictions inherent in the human condition, forcing audiences to confront the complexity of their own disgust.

Compassion

Central to this methodology is the unwavering thread of compassion that runs through even the darkest narratives. This approach recognises the power of theatre to delve into the depths of human suffering, loss and despair, yet it insists that these explorations are always grounded in empathy. Compassion becomes the guiding light, ensuring that no matter how deep the narrative plunges into darkness, there remains a beacon of hope and humanity, and that kindness prevails.

The existential approach

Existentialism, with its focus on individual agency, the absurdity of life, and the human condition, provides a solid philosophical backdrop to this work. By incorporating existentialist questions and dilemmas, the theatre becomes a space where the complexities of human freedom, choice, and the inherent search for meaning are vividly brought to life, pushing all involved to confront the most fundamental aspects of what it means to be human in this universe and the quest for authenticity amidst life's inherent uncertainties.

A plea for authenticity

The Sensitised Theatre is more than a methodology; it's a plea for authenticity and compassion in an era of disconnection. It's a strategy for reclaiming the transformative power of theatre, to celebrate our shared humanity and to navigate the complexities of life with empathy, compassion and openness, urging us to turn beautifully towards our own discomfort.

This is my vision for a revived British theatre, one that not only reflects the tumult of our times, but also offers a beacon of hope and community. As we move forward, let's challenge ourselves to break free from the confines of traditional theatre and explore the boundless possibilities of human expression and connection.

Good fucking luck,

Adam Scott-Rowley
London, March 2024

Acknowledgements

To my family, for their love, sense of humour and for not suppressing strangeness.

To Oliver Wellington, for his unwavering love, support and encouragement.

To Joseph Prowen and Tom Morley, for their extraordinary patience, silliness, and the occasional good idea.

To Matt Cater, for his gorgeous design, inventiveness and pre-show checks.

To Gill Cuthbertson, for teaching me and for introducing me to the avant-garde.

To Julie Carlsen and my colleagues and students at Den Danske Scenekunstskole, for giving me the opportunity and resources to develop these ideas.

To Jeremy Zimmermann, for his kindness, madness and charm.

To my LAMDA friends, for putting up with me.

To Colin Blumenau and The Production Exchange, for taking a risk.

To Torben Dahl, for getting me to Denmark.

And finally to Edward Halsted, Will Scarnell and everyone who supported the early stages of my work, both financially and otherwise, without whom none of this would have been possible.

YOU ARE GOING TO DIE

Originally presented with one actor, but it could be many.

Good instincts merit a loosening of the text.

Hold the space with compassion.

To be performed naked.

Dreamlike.

Stark. A naked figure is sitting on a toilet. They are in silent meditation.

They bring awareness to their feelings and to the audience. There is an air of devotion, yet it is mischievous.

A figure brings their hands to their face, as if wiping away several masks.

A figure is standing.

A figure is rocking on a precipice.

A figure clutches the corpse of their child to their chest.

A figure uncomfortable in their own skin.

A figure showing dominance.

A figure soothes themselves.

A figure is demented.

A figure in awe.

A figure, sinister, beckons.

A figure is impish, also beckoning, playful with the audience.

A figure reveals their arsehole.

A figure in a corner, cries alone.

*A **Macho Figure** is birthed. They are built like a brick shit house and riddled with tension, trying desperately to hide their pain. As the tension becomes too much, they drop this hollow exterior, caught off guard by their own inauthenticity. This gives space to **Root Figure**, who is softer, more vulnerable, not performing. They allow their embarrassment to show. **Macho Figure** punishes themself for this. Tries harder. They flex their muscles. They peacock. **Macho Figure** will do anything to suppress the honesty of **Root Figure**.*

Macho Figure   B-B-B-B-BLOKE! B-B-B-B-BLOKE! BLOKE!

Macho Figure's *tension becomes ridiculously exaggerated. A bullish dominance; they're not taking any prisoners. Are they human or gorilla? Animalistic grunts mingle with the moans of a power-bottom. They go further.* **Root Figure**, *ashamed, surfaces again. Then,* **Macho Figure** *notices the toilet. They want to fuck it but dare they approach such porcelain majesty?*

Slowly, **Macho Figure**, *genuflecting like a mediaeval serf, approaches the toilet until everything, including character, falls away. A moment of shared vulnerability with the audience.*

A figure is sitting on the toilet.

A figure slowly contorts, taking on the aches, pains and wisdom of an old body.

Curious Figure   My little pussy's in heaven. Funny the joy a little thing like that can bring into one's life. I loved her with all my heart. You know, it was sort of hauntingly beautiful, watching her final days. I remember – I moved her basket to her favourite spot in front of the fire and she'd just lie there from morning to night. I put my nose to hers, it was as dry as a bone! I could hear her poor laboured breathing . . .

Curious Figure *breathes like a dying cat.*

What was running through that little mind? Those eyes . . . Ha! Those eyes . . . So serene, even in all that pain. Of course she knew. She was teaching me. What an extraordinary pussy cat – to meet the precipice like that, with such courage. I do wonder what she'll come back as. Perhaps a bird. I think she would very much enjoy soaring high above the mountains.

A cat purrs and cleans their ears.

Demented Figure, *frail, on a stage, joyfully reliving the memory of a performance long finished. They are singing an old song with a tap routine.*

Darkness.

A shaft of light appears and they are drawn to it, like a moth.

Darkness.

A shaft of light appears and they are drawn to it, like a moth.

Darkness.

A shaft of light appears and they are drawn to it, like a moth.

Existential Figure *is stuck in a well. They'll do anything to get the audience's attention.*

Existential Figure   Oh my god. I think I'm stuck in a well. Tell me you're stuck in a well without telling me you're stuck in a well.

They touch the well wall.

Euurghhhh! Slimy! Fuck! Hahaha.

Pause. What else might the audience want?

Oh my god – tell me you're cold without telling me you're cold.

They start to shiver. It is performative and fake.

The shivering slowly becomes real. They are actually stuck in a well. Panic.

Oh my god. I think I'm actually stuck in a well. Fuck, fuck . . . What the actual fuck?! Oh my god! Don't panic. Just focus on your breathing. Fuck! Help! Mum? Dad? I'm stuck in the well!

Blackout. Thunder. Heavy rain.

Private and barely visible:

A figure is standing.

A figure is rocking on a precipice.

A figure clutches the corpse of their child to their chest.

A figure uncomfortable in their own skin.

A figure showing dominance.

A figure soothes themselves.

A figure is demented.

A figure in awe.

A figure is rocking on a precipice.

A moment of stillness.

An impending ritual.

Imp Figure *is in a frenzy. Brutal. Volatile. Horrifying. The universal embodiment of the inevitability of suffering.*

They dance. They scream. They reveal their arsehole.

They circumambulate the toilet, which is now a boiling cauldron. They are summoning something.

Moments before its climax, the ritual gives way to:

Avuncular Figure*. Obese. Terminally ill. Retching into the toilet. A glint in their eye.*

They address the audience directly.

Avuncular Figure   Fucking hell . . . Everyone OK? Right . . . how are we all? Relaxed? Sitting soft? Enjoying yourselves? Good. No, no, that's good.

Hello, love, so what do you think happens when we die?

Avuncular Figure *listens and responds playfully. They move on:*

I tell you what, ladies and gents, if there's one thing that all of us here tonight have in common, is that none of us has a clue what's going on. Just over eight billion souls on this planet and not a single one of us has even the slightest clue! Not a fucking carrot!

Right here's one for ya . . . Mother-in-laws . . . mother-in-laws. I were round my mother-in-law's last Sunday for dinner. Had fire going, just had our tea, sitting in lounge afterwards. Telly's on, kids playing. Everyone's half-cut, you know . . . and I caught my mother-in-law's gaze from across the room, just briefly. And she had this strange look in her eye. So I locked eyes with her. Stared at her. Straight down fucking barrel. And I just thought to myself . . . Christ. You've done so much for me. You've been like a mother to me.

Pause.

You see my wife died five years ago, and my mother-in-law still treats me like family. And I think, since my wife's death, I've been searching to feel like I belonged, searching to feel at home, really . . . and I found it – that Sunday afternoon in your gaze. First person to teach me about self care, my mother-in-law – and fucking hell did I need it! I'd never speak to anyone now the way I used to speak to myself. I've been a nasty BASTARD in my time. I've been closed off, cruel, I've been afraid. Afraid to be open. And you know . . . it makes you old before your time, it makes you stagnate. Makes you sick. 'Self care? FUCK OFF', I used to think. But then when she really explained it, I realised – it's not about being sickly sweet, wearing hemp, lighting candles and being a WANKER. It's about taking courage and turning towards your pain, opening yourself up to new experiences, new perspectives. She taught me that at some point you've just got to say YES to life. I've said yes to so much recently. It wasn't until last week, I was on my bathroom floor, knee pads on, slipping and sliding all over the place, with a dildo, so deep inside me it's given me whooping cough, that I thought . . . YES. I've made some bloody positive changes in my life – I mean don't get me wrong – I'm still a sad bastard, but if my wife was here now, I think she'd be proud of me. So I've written a little ditty, a little song, to say thank you. (*To someone offstage.*) Hit it, love.

Heavy rain.

A figure is rocking on a precipice.

Grieving Figure *comes in from the rain.*[1]

Grieving Figure   Iesu mawr . . . Dwi 'di cael uffer' o ddiwrnod. One hell of a day. Y glaw 'di o. Melltith mam Gaia yw hi. This bloody rain! Chwech oen da ni 'di colli wythnos yma – six lambs we've lost . . . Roeddwn i fyny yn yr ysgubor uchaf – fixing the tarpaulin – pan glywais y swnian 'ma y tu ôl i mi. Edrychais tuag at y wal gefn a gweld bêl wen fach 'ma o fflwff gyda'i choesau i gyd wedi'u troelli a'u torri. Mae'n rhaid bod o wedi llithro – it must have slipped . . . Es i ato. Edrychais i fyny ar yr awyr. Y blydi glaw 'ma. Bwrw hen wragedd a ffyn. Bechod. Nes i strôcio ei ben a wedyn ymestyn i mewn i fy mhoced cefn. Ffyc. Fy nghyllell. My knife. Nes i strôcio ei ben bach eto ac yna tynhau fy ngafael o amgylch gwddf yr oen. Roedd yn rhyfadd ond doedd gen i ddim llawer o ddewis na? I dagu peth bach felly. My poor little lamb . . . Does dim byd tebyg i'r foment pan mae'r bywyd yn . . . There's nothing quite like the moment when you see the life . . .

Grieving Figure *is strangling a lamb.*

Grieving Figure *clutches the corpse of their child to their chest.*

A silent scream into the abyss.

Imp Figure *beckons.*

Existential Figure *is dancing in a club.*

---

[1] **Grieving Figure**'s *dialogue is to be performed in a language not often heard in the area where the play is being presented. They can occasionally offer a phrase in English.*

Grieving Figure (*translation*)   Jesus Christ! I've had one hell of a day. One hell of a day. It's the rain. It's Mother Gaia's curse. This bloody rain! Six lambs we've lost this week . . . I was up in the top barn fixing the tarpaulin – when I heard this sound behind me. I looked towards the back wall and saw this small ball of white fluff with its legs all twisted and broken. It must have slipped . . . I approached. I looked up towards the sky. This bloody rain. Raining cats and dogs. Poor thing. I stroked its head, and then reached into my back pocket. Fuck. My knife. I stroked its little head again and then tightened my hand around the lamb's throat. It was strange, but I didn't have much of a choice, did I? To strangle a little thing like that. My poor little lamb . . . There's nothing quite like the moment when the life is . . . There's nothing quite like the moment when you see the life . . .

Existential Figure Oh my GOD! Tell me you're having fun without telling me you're having fun.

Existential Figure *dances offensively. The well slowly encloses them.*

Existential Figure (*inaudible to the audience*) WHAT THE FUCK?!

Imp Figure *torments* **Existential Figure**. **Existential Figure** *suppresses.*

Appalling. Awful. Dreadful.

Imp Figure *prevails, bursting out of the well. The well disappears.*

Imp Figure *dances, screams, reveals their arsehole.*

Macho Figure *oozes into the club, on the hunt. They clock the toilet. Your majesty.*

On the approach, brimming with anticipation:

Macho Figure Ohhh. Just look at you, you glorious porcelain beauty. Ooh . . . may I approach? Ahh such majesty. Please, tell me, tell me, for I need to know: just how deep those porcelain waters flow? Let me plunge myself into your holy depths.

They lie prostrate at the foot of the bowl.

May I rim you, your Majesty? Please let me rim your regal rim. Let me rim-ya-rim? Rimyarimyarimyarimrimrimrimrimrim! Let this lowly peasant-worm clean you. Let me bring back that sacred skleen.

They rim the rim.

Root Figure *is vomited into the light. They are deeply humiliated.*

Root Figure I'm sorry. I'm so so sorry. What am I doing?

Macho Figure SHUT UP, YOU FUCKING CUNT!

Root Figure *is crying.* **Macho Figure** *returns to his idol, savagely rimming:*

Macho Figure   Ayyyuuyuuhh! I'm gunna fucking cum! YOU. ARE. MAKING. ME. CUMMMMM!

The orgasm of a thousand lifetimes. It becomes aggressive, out of control.

Suddenly, it's a baroque courtly dance. A grotesque révérence.

Fank you. Oh fank you. Fank you. Fanking you.

This persists, outstaying its welcome, they collapse.

Forgive me, your Majesty. Forgive me for I am nothing. I'm a rat, I'm mud, I'm ooze, I'm shit cum chav, I'm scum, I'm a pleb, I'm a serf, I'm a peasant. Peasant, peasant, peasant, peasant rat ooze shit cuckold! I'M A FUCKING CUCK! I'm NOTHING! I'm smaller than a dandelion! I'm a lowly WORM.

As pathetic as it gets:

(*Lullabying*) I'm a lowly worm. I'm a lowly worm. Shit snot cum cuck cuck cuckadoodledoo-cuckadoodledoo! I'm a fucking chicken. (*Rebuilding.*) I'm a fucking rooster! I'm an animal. I'm a gorilla, I'm a man, I'm machine, I'm metal, I'm bite, I'm snake, I'm MONEY, I'm BOSH! (*Animalistic.*) I'm UUUERH! (*Hyper-sexualised.*) I'm EUURRRGHAAAA! (*Rampant.*) I'm THE KING! I'm top of the food chain and I'm taking up all the fucking SPACE! YOU CUNT!

Silence.

Macho Figure & Root Figure   There's something wrong with you. There's something seriously fucking wrong with you.

Silence.

Root Figure *soothes themself.*

Curious Figure *is sitting on the toilet. They are lost in thought.*

Curious Figure   Funny how fear torments us. And yet the more I run away from it the more it seems to overwhelm me. It has me in its grip. My numbered days are completely consumed by the fear . . . that my days are numbered! I'm embarrassed to say, it's got to the point where I don't know where the fear ends and I begin! And even in those rare moments of freedom when I'm not afraid, I find myself worrying about when the fear might return. Something I'm investigating – just the rudiments of course – is the sensation of fear itself. What the bloody hell is it? Well, it's sweaty palms, a tight knot in the pit of the stomach, a racing heartbeat – and of course it's so unpleasant, I want to resist it – it's painful. But if I resist it . . . it's like stoking a fire. So, what if I am able to accept that it is there, without resistance? What if I turn towards my pain? Then I am granted a spaciousness around the fear, in which I can be curious . . . I wonder what it will be like? To sway on the precipice of oblivion?

Curious Figure *brings their hands to their face, as if wiping away several masks.*

The actor/s are left bare in the nakedness of the moment. There is a liveness, a vulnerability, an accepting quality. For some moments we are not sure who is the observer and who is the observed. The dream of the play seems like a distant memory.

Gently, we return:

Curious Figure   Now I don't know about you, but thinking about all this gives me the willies. That dreadful awe! Thank goodness it ebbs and flows. Imagine . . . to be constantly full of awe . . . awful! Very curious, isn't it, bringing fear into the light.

Demented Figure *returns to their stage, coming in and out of lucidity.*

Their routine comes back to them in fragments. They're losing grip. An increscent nothingness.

In an attempt to hold on to the self, a frenzied scramble of emotion and expression.

Desperate. Mean and grasping.

Anything but oblivion.

From this darkness, **Imp Figure** *beckons.*

Existential Figure *is back in the well.*

Existential Figure   Oh my god . . . Fuck. Tell me you're trying to overcome your existential anxiety without telling me you're trying to overcome your existential anxiety.

They ready themself to escape the well.

They do it.

They can't quite believe it. Can it really be that easy?

They look back at the well.

Oh my god. I'm out of the well. So easy . . . Fuck!

They look back again, the well is gone. Their stomach drops.

Oh my god. I'm out of my well. Ermmm . . . Tell me you're . . . that you love, tell me you're loved without telling me you're . . . Don't you just love to see it when I'm . . .? Don't you just love to see to see when I love to see when I ermmm when I . . . when I'm . . . stuck . . . when I'm stuck in cyclic thinking? Do you love . . . do you . . . do you . . . ermmm . . . Tell me you're loved without show me you're love –

An intrusive memory. Looming parental shadows. Distorted:

Father Figure   Why is my *Financial Times* completely bloody sopping wet?

Mother Figure   Don't ask me, ask your daughter, she was running around with it all day.

Father Figure   That little bitch!

Mother Figure   She's bored out of her mind – and she's only here for two weeks of the bloody year!

Father Figure   Well, if she's bored out of her bloody mind it's because you don't keep her entertained.

Mother Figure   Oh! It's my job, is it?

Father Figure   Of course it's your bloody job, because I have an actual job, an actual job, an actual job, in the city . . . your job seems to be sitting around all day drinking Pinot FUCKING Grigio.

Beat.

Mother Figure   How dare you! How dare you! You haven't looked at her since the day she was born.

Father Figure   Well, I never wanted her in the first place!

Mother Figure   Of course you didn't, because she's not yours, is she? Because you were firing blanks!

Father Figure   Don't you bloody dare! Rather it was the sight of you turning me sick! That's why I fucked the au pair!

Beat.

Mother Figure   Well . . . I've been fucking your brother for years!

Father Figure   Oh bra-fucking-va! There isn't anyone in Chelsea he hasn't bloody fucked!

Mother Figure   You disgust me! You disgust me! You disgust me! I wish I'd never met you!

Father Figure   And I wish that little bitch had never been born!

Mother Figure   WELL AT LEAST THAT'S ONE THING WE CAN FUCKING AGREE ON!

Existential Figure *silently screams. Everything is wiped clean.*

The fabric of reality starts to fall apart.

Grieving Figure *finds themself on a hillside. Eyes staring back from the darkness. Dread and foreboding.*

Grieving Figure   Tud laen wan ci bach![2]

They whistle for their dog.

They stick their finger in their mouth then hold it up to the wind.

They check for rain.

They whistle again.

They look up at the gathering storm clouds.

Tud laen wan ci bach! Tud![3]

They reach for their child's hand.

Emptiness.

Grief hits them like a truck.

With a mighty force, on the precipice of extinction:

Grieving Figure *clutches the corpse of their child to their chest.*

They are liberated.

Existential Figure *uncomfortable in their own skin.*

They are liberated.

Masculine Figure *showing dominance.*

They are liberated.

Root Figure *soothes themself.*

They are liberated.

Demented Figure *is terrified.*

They are liberated.

---

[2] *Translation:* **Grieving Figure**   Come on now, little dog!
[3] *Translation:* **Grieving Figure**   Come on now, little dog! Come!

Curious Figure *is in awe. Heart open to the heavens.*

Curious Figure   Yes!

They are liberated.

They collapse.

Exhausted, they drag themselves towards the toilet.

Silence.

A figure, with their head in the bowl, breathing.

Avuncular Figure   Fucking hell. I am absolutely shattered!
Don't worry, love, five more minutes and we can all have a
drink. Right, where was I . . .? Oh yes, my song! Hit it, love.

A dystopian cabaret at the end of the world. A grand finale:

> I'm tired, I'm fucked up
> Left all alone, on my knees
> Covered in throw-up and shite
> My skin stinks like rotting poultry
> But I've a dildo hanging out my arse
>
> Christ I've known better days
> How did things come to this?
> It couldn't have turned out much worse if I'd tried
>
> But when all is said and done
> D'ya know what love . . .
> Christ we've had some bloody good fun
>
> So don't be cruel to yourself
> Everyone here feels pain
> Trust me it's nothing new
> I've had a few knocks myself
>
> So turn towards your pain
> Bloody hell I know it's hard
> Whatever you feel, just know you're not alone

Just take a look at sad old me
With a dildo hanging out my arse

You are not your pain
It doesn't define who you are
So come on now
Be here together
You are love
You are only love
None of this will matter much
When you're dead and return to the stars

What else is there to do, my love
What else is there to feel
When I'm alone on my knees
With a dildo – a great big dildo
Just hanging out my arse

So why do we
Waste our time
Feeling anxious and afraid
I said why do we
Fucking waste our time
Holding grudges all our lives
When we could all just be having fun
With a great big dildo stuck up our bums

It's a dildo (Hanging out my arse)
Dildo (Hanging out my arse)
It's a dildo yeah (Hanging out my arse)
Great big dildo yeah (Hanging out my arse)
Rainbow dildo yeah (Hanging out my arse)
Made in China yeah (Hanging out my arse)
Dildo dildo D-I-L-D-O it's a dildo! Yeah!

Turn towards your pain
Fucking hell I know it's hard
Whatever you feel just know you're not alone
Just take a look at sad old me
With a dildo hanging out my arse

You are not your pain
It doesn't define who you are
So come on now
Be here together
Have a glass of wine
Have a bloody good laugh
You are love
You are only love
None of this will matter much
When you're dead and return to the stars!

The song ends. We are suspended between the dream of the play and the reality of the space we are in. Intrusively sober.

Is there more to say?

Ends.

THIS IS NOT CULTURALLY
SIGNIFICANT

A play created for one actor, but do with it what you will.

The dialogue offered is a somewhat mangled suggestion of tone and context. Use as much or as little of it as you see fit.

Energetic and rhythmic, with an all pervading anger. Should feel like torture from start to finish.

Pay no heed to gender.

To be performed naked.

Give the audience what they need, not necessarily what they want.

The following are nightmarish caricatures:

Figure, *the blank canvas, on which everything appears. At times neutral, but often distressed and confused.*

American Pornstar, *a grotesque concentration of an over-sexualised female form, revoltingly conceptualised through a misogynistic gaze.*

American Pornstar's Father, *a typically unemotional man in the winter of his life. Churchgoing and pained over his past but without the self-awareness to process it. He is gentle but with an air of melancholy. Should feel as though he is from another era. His lines are always sung and melodramatic.*

Glaswegian Woman, *the sad embodiment of how right-wing politics leaves the most vulnerable in society behind. An appalling state of affairs. Miraculously, she maintains a good sense of humour and mischievousness. Making the best she can of a terrible situation.*

Mendacious Lecturer, *angry academic living in a world that has left him behind. A confused know-it-all with a superiority complex. He has dysprosody. Awful temper.*

Clubrat, *a toxic cocktail of self-adoration, protecting a lonely and terrified vulnerability. Occasionally their mask slips and we see a glimpse of their most awful inner sadness.*

Dennis, *the personification of toxic masculinity and violence. He is rage. He is a wife-beater. Fucking horrendous to be around. He was* *never offered the support, nor had the courage needed, to meet his pain.*

Miriam, *if only she'd never met Dennis, she could have lived a good life. Physically frail and always shivering. She's like a cracked vase. Defeated but hanging on by a thread. Extraordinary how she can keep going in the face of such adversity. Has a dark side.*

Grieving Widow, *if grief were a person, she would look like this. Graceful, haunting and beautiful.*

Love_me, *weapons-grade nightmare. They absolutely live off attention, whilst pretending to hate it. As insecure as they come. In need of compassion – if only they existed in a kinder world.*

The Gentleman's Keeper, *snob. Arched. Chairman of the board.*

Torycunt, *self-explanatory.*

Theatre Landlord, *owns half the West End. If old fashioned theatricality could be encapsulated in a body. Yearns for a time long passed, his years of experience being the only thing keeping him from obsolescence. He has every health problem under the sun, uses an oxygen tank from years of smoking cigars, and can barely get through a sentence without coughing and gasping. His tracheostomy makes his throat sound like it's farting.*

Fartclown, *is a fucking idiot. They're relentless. A horrid little child. Will do anything to undermine.*

Dingy. Centre stage, a simple piece of set, such as a stool. A hanging industrial light nearby.

A **Figure** *appears out of breath, deeply distressed. Where are they and what the fuck is going on? Will the audience offer them any help?*

The mood bleeds into something voyeuristic and we are confronted with **American Pornstar**. *She's a camgirl. Depressing and hypnotically demonstrative, she's facing the audience, fucking herself.*

American Pornstar   Oh my god! Did my pussy just tell me that there was a party tonight? I'm such a dirty bitch . . . and I've got a nasty habit!

She winces as she starts to play with her clit.

Oh my shit! Oh my dirty little shit-fuck! This stool is so good for my pussy! Oh it's good for my pussy . . . Oh my god! Oh my . . .

She falls silent then orgasms. It's wonderfully grotesque.

Oh my fucking cunt, this stool is making me so wet! It's so good for my darn pussy!

As if birthed from **American Pornstar**'s *vagina,* **American Pornstar's Father** *appears.*

American Pornstar's Father
   I've been sittin' on my porch for one year now,
   Waiting here all alone . . .
   I've been sittin' on my porch for one year now,
   Waiting for my daughter to come home . . .

Glaswegian Woman *bursts out of his song.*

It's cold and pissing it down. She is homeless and life has been far too cruel. She's on the brink of losing her sanity. She is being provoked by an unseen police officer.

Glaswegian Woman   Get your fucking hands off of me!
This is police brutality at its worst . . . Fucking PIG! What
have I done now . . . Officer?

Beat.

You know this is my spot!

Beat.

I have not been smoking cannabis! At least not today . . .
(*Mischievously.*) It gives my brain the silly buggers . . .

A contortion.

Sober. A lecture hall with **Mendacious Lecturer***.*

Mendacious Lecturer   Good evening, ladies and
gentlemen and thank you all for coming here tonight. I am
very honoured indeed to be here and I am thoroughly
looking forward to the Q and A, after the lecture. I do hope
that you are all sitting comfortably, and remember, if you see
anything or anyone behaving suspiciously, then please
report it to myself, a member of the university staff . . . or
indeed, a police officer. SEE IT! SAY IT! SORTED!

Beat.

Now. If you think that dying is anything other than going
home, then you've been kidding yourselves! How in this
modern age are we to maintain a spiritualist outlook?

Beat.

You see, spiritualism . . . transcends politics . . . Spiritualism
transcends historical study . . . And spiritualism . . .
transcends . . . culture. What happens when one . . . has
reached this . . . what happens . . . transcendental point of
STUDY!

Silence.

. . . I hear you ask? Well, the spirit comes OUT . . . and you
. . . play!

Beat.

Now, I'm not some pseudo-spiritual MAGICIAN! How dare you? There is not a single Buddhist or Hindu text that I have not read . . .

Silence.

Of course I don't mind, always happy to oblige! CONGREGATION CONGREGATION! I like to play a little game.

Beat.

. . . I'm swimming . . .

Beat.

Somebody name me an obscure Buddhist . . . or Hindu . . . TEXT.

They do. If they don't, wait. In response:

You've just made a very, VERY powerful enemy!

An LGBTQIA+ nightclub, music blasting. The rhythm introduces us to **Clubrat**. *They're dancing.*

Clubrat (*rhythmically*)
    S S S Sorry love, it's not my problem . . .
    S S S Sorry love, it's not my problem . . .
    S S S Sorry love, it's not my problem . . .
    S S S Sorry love, it's not my problem.
    I'm on the Spectrum![1]

A basement flat beneath the nightclub. Its inhabitants are looming. Out of **Clubrat**'s *dancing,* **Dennis** *is banging on the ceiling.*

Dennis   Fucking faggots in that club upstairs playing that fucking faggoty music!

Breakneck transitions. Like a lightning strike.

---

[1] **Clubrat** is not neurodivergent, however, they will happily tell everyone they are for attention. 'I'm on the Spectrum' could be updated to a relevant comment of the same effect.

Miriam   Dennis! You mustn't use words like that!

Dennis   Shut your fucking mouth, you fat pig!

Miriam   Dennis . . . Why is your face so red?

Dennis   I've just had a shit, and I had to splash myself with water to cool down.

Miriam   Oh Dennis . . . that's disgusting!

Dennis   SHUT UP! What's for dinner?

Miriam   Beans, Dennis . . . You know that's about all we can afford these days.

Beat.

(*Singing sweetly.*) Beans beans they're good for your heart . . .

Dennis   Get in the kitchen, you ungrateful tart!

Miriam *quivers into:*

A dusty music hall, perhaps in her mind, perhaps in her home, **Grieving Widow** *is holding the hanging light as if it's a microphone. Haunting and uneasy.*

Grieving Widow   Graze, Danke.

Pause.

The ladies down at the club are almost completely convinced that I've got depression. Although I'm sure that's not the case . . . I just . . . miss waking up next to you, Bernie. Recently, I can hardly find the courage to get out of bed, and when I do manage it, my days just feel so empty . . .

Beat.

Grieving Widow   Oh Bernie. This one's for you . . .

She sings a song. Yearning, sad, pretty.

As if falling, back on the street:

Glaswegian Woman   The joke's on you, Officer! I'd be quite happy to spend a night in the cell. Anything to keep me away from the foxes and the pigeon shite!

Beat.

Ah, Officer . . . are you looking at my legs?

An elongation into:

Love_Me, *a camera-obsessed influencer, talks to the audience. They are post-coitally flirting and posing with an unseen partner who is filming them.*

Love_Me   Oh my god . . . You don't think they look fat do you? No babe, but like seriously, do you think my legs look fat? Oh my god, you're such a fucker! Turn it off! No but like you are . . . hahaha you're such a fucker! (*Still playful.*) You cunt! Stop filming me!

Beat. Something shifts. It turns nasty.

What's wrong with it?

Beat.

Alright fine . . . I'll get changed . . . Don't film me when I'm getting –

Legs akimbo:

American Pornstar, *working the sexcams, distracted on the phone to her father.*

American Pornstar   – changed, Daddy. I can't really talk.

On the other end of the line:

American Pornstar's Father
   Oh my darling girl, it's good to hear your voice.
   I'm so proud of you, you've made such a brave choice.
   Since your mother died, I've been so awful lonely.
   Eating my meals alone and waiting for you to phone me.

American Pornstar   Oh Daddy, you're so cute . . . I'll call you next week, my show's about to start . . . Daddy, I've really gotta go!

American Pornstar's Father
   Okay my darlin' girl,
   But tell me, what's the show?

American Pornstar   Uhhhh it's a cabaret . . . Daddy!

She hangs up.

American Pornstar's Father
   I've been sittin' on my porch for five years now,
   Waiting here all alone.
   I've been sittin' on my porch for five years now,
   Waiting for my daughter to come –

Lurch into **Dennis** *and* **Miriam***'s flat. The club's still pounding upstairs.*

Dennis   – in here you stupid bitch! Why don't you clean up around here anymore?!

Miriam   Dennis, I'm working three jobs! When I get home I've barely got time to put me feet up!

Dennis   Where's my DINNER?!

Miriam   Don't shout at me! I'll get it for you now, Dennis . . .

Dennis   Bring it into the computer room . . . I'm watching my sexcams tonight!

Back to the sexcams:

American Pornstar   Okay . . . Let's get this show on the road . . . Who's online tonight . . . Dennis-Underscore-HardCock-Underscrore-DaddyFuck?

The locations switch rapidly:

Dennis   Urrghh yeah . . . You're a nasty little tart, aren't ya . . . That's it! Keep going . . . keep going for Dennis!

American Pornstar   Yeah . . . do ya like that, Daddy? Mmmmm do ya like that Dennis-Underscore-HardCock-Underscrore-DaddyFuck?

Dennis   Phwoar! I do like that!

American Pornstar   Well, Dennis . . . You're making me so wet! Mmmmm I'm gunna fucking squirt!

Dennis   Oh yeah . . . Squirt on the camera, baby, squirt on the FUCKING camera –

Street-level, outside the LGBTQIA+ club. **The Gentleman's Keeper** *is managing the queue.*

The Gentleman's Keeper (*rhythmically*)
  S S S Sorry Madam – you can't.
  S S S Sorry Madam, you can't come in.
  For this, HA! HA! HA!
  This, HA! HA! HA!
  This, is, The Gentleman's Club!

Inside the club, **Clubrat** *is still dancing.*

Clubrat
  S S S Sorry love, it's not my problem . . .
  S S S Sorry love, it's not my problem.
  I'm on the Spectrum!

Outside:

The Gentleman's Keeper
  S S S Sorry Madam – you can't.
  S S S Sorry Madam, you can't come in.
  For this, HA! HA! HA!
  This, HA! HA! HA!
  This, is, The Gentleman's Club!

Inside:

Clubrat
  S S S Sorry love, it's not my problem.
  I'm on the Spectrum!

Where's my coke stash?! Have you seen my coke stash?!

A liminal space:

Figure (*What the fuck is happening to me?*)

A possession into:

A living room. **Torycunt** *is on her soapbox, talking to the audience.*

Torycunt   Well yes, darling . . . I know I'm not alone when I say I'm becoming increasingly worried with the amount of **ILLEGAL IMMIGRANTS** we are allowing into this country . . . I mean, only recently we had a bunch of them take over the local shop . . . didn't we, Hugo?

Beat.

Hugo . . .

Beat.

HUGO! Put that down! And pull those up, will you . . . it's quite unflattering.

Beat.

What was that man's name again? Taken over the shop.

Beat.

Yes you do know who I'm talking about, darling . . . the little foreign one from the shop on the corner . . .

Beat.

Yes you do!

Beat.

With that great big bloody you-know-whatsit-thing on his head! He's . . . Strong smell of incense. Grubby floors.

Beat.

Ah yes! That's it . . . Aharharharharhar . . . His name's
ACHCHCHCHCHCHCHCHCHCHCHCHCHCHCHCMED!
And the other one is called ACHCHCHCHCHCHCHCHCH-

Bleeds into an ugly and painful coughing fit.

Suddenly, London's glamorous and glittering West End:

Theatre Landlord   Thank you for all congregating here in
London's wonderful Drury Lane. As I'm sure some of you
are already aware, we have been given our notice to vacate
the theatre, by the end of this week.

Beat.

Now, as far as I'm concerned, it's been a BLOODY good
season of theatre, and dare I say, some of the best I've ever
produced. Who could have predicted the extraordinary
success of Chekhov's lesser known works, such as 'Ivanov',
'Platonov', 'Turnthatlightov', 'Takethatbraov', and my
personal favourite, 'FUCKOV'![2]

Beat.

So it is with great sadness that I inform you all now, that in
five days' time, Andrew Lloyd FUCKING Webber's moving
in.

Unfortunately, **Fartclown** *arrives.*

*They clown with the audience, refusing to leave until everyone in the
audience is joining in with call and response fart noises.*

Glaswegian Woman*'s just shat herself.*

Glaswegian Woman   Whoopsie! Excuse me, Officer . . . Ah!

Beat.

You're still looking at my legs! Do y'know, Officer, I loved
ballet when I was a wee girl . . .

Beat.

---

[2] Forgive us, we know these jokes are pathetic.

(*Practising her plié.*) Knees over the toes, knees over the toes!

Losing balance, back to the cams:

Dennis   Phwoar, that's it, SLUT, keep going!

Supersonic speed in the transitions, without rushing the caricatures:

American Pornstar   Oh yeah, d'ya like that Dennis-Underscore-HardCock-Underscrore-DaddyFuck?

Dennis   I do . . . I do . . .

Coming from the kitchen:

Miriam   Dennis, I've got your baked bean dinner here . . .

Dennis   Put it on the floor, you daft pig.

American Pornstar   Ohh who's that, Dennis? Your wife? Has she come to join the pussy-party?

Dennis   It's no one – keep going.

American Pornstar   Oh okay, Dennis . . . You're gunna make my thistle . . . whistle.

Dennis   BLOODY HELL! What else am I gunna do?

American Pornstar   Mmmmmm . . . You're gunna make my petunia . . .

Beat.

American Pornstar   Peculiar?

Dennis   Oh FUCK! Why don't you call me Daddy?

American Pornstar   Oh! Okay, Daddy . . . Daddy! Daddy! Daddy! DiddlydoodooDaddy!

Her phone is ringing.

. . . Daddy! Daddy? (*Picking up the phone.*) Oh Daddy, hi!

American Pornstar's Father
   Oh my darlin' girl,
   I've been trying get through for weeks,
   It's so good to hear your voice –

Dennis   Now spread those FUCKING cheeks!

American Pornstar   Oh don't you worry, Daddy, I'm coming real soon!

American Pornstar's Father
You've put a smile on an old man's face . . .

Miriam   Dennis, have you seen the broom?

Miriam, *entering the computer room, notices* **American Pornstar** *on the sexcam.*

Beat.

Miriam   Dennis! Can she can see us?! Dennis! No, that's horrible . . . that's disgusting . . . that's . . . that's not live, is it?

Dennis   Fuck off, pig-breath! How can I cum when you're staring at me like a fucking CORPSE?

American Pornstar   Oh my god, I'm gunna cum . . . Oh my god, I'm gunna fucking burst!

Dennis   Come on, love, get me going, get me going!

Miriam *frozen to the spot. Inconsolable.*

American Pornstar *climaxing.*

Miriam *crying.*

American Pornstar *climaxing.*

This reaches a profound intensity, becoming a guttural expression of woe.

A mother searching for her young across a desert landscape.

American Pornstar *and* **Miriam** *somewhere between climaxing and a screaming grief.*

American Pornstar *finishes.*

American Pornstar's **Father** *is still on the end of the line, listening to all of this. He puts the phone down slowly, unsure of what's just happened.*

American Pornstar's Father
   I've been sittin' on my porch for ten years now,
   Waiting here all alone . . .
   I've been sittin' on my porch for ten years now,
   Waiting for my daughter to come home . . .

Startled:

Grieving Widow   Bernie, is that you?

Beat.

I've been doing this dreadful thing recently where I catch
sight of the back of a stranger's head, or the side of
someone's face on a passing bus, and for a split second I'm
convinced . . . utterly convinced that it's you, Bernie . . .

Beat.

But of course . . . That would be impossible. God I miss you
so much . . .

Beat.

This one's . . . for myself . . .

*She sings a beautifully eerie and timeless song about love and
connection – prematurely, we fall again. Further this time:*

Glaswegian Woman   My children?! I haven't seen them
since you lot took them away from me.

Beat.

You're alright, you . . . I've seen the way you look at me, Off –

A moment of suspension.

The **Figure** *is frozen in limbo, naked and vulnerable.*

Dissociated. All has decayed. Are we in a simulation? No, too raw.

Glaswegian Woman   – icer! Who could blame you for
taking a liking to me? A lady with such decorum . . .

Beat.

Hey, Officer . . . d'ya wanna fuck me . . . Officer?

Beat.

Huh? D'ya wanna put your truncheon right up my bot? Do you, Officer? D'ya wanna feel it slip and slide inside my botpussy?

She's provocatively bent over, belting her arse. She falls forwards coughing:

Theatre Landlord   And of course this significant lack of taste, and profound decline in the quality of British theatre, has led us all to ask some rather pertinent questions . . .

Beat.

Must we continue to rely on slapstick-ridden, narrative-driven, text-based theatre?

The caricatures are starting to bleed together:

Mendacious Lecturer   Why waste your time with such trivial matters as the theatre? The only theatre we should really be interested in, is the theatre of the mind! Take this question for example . . . What are . . . DREAMS?

A moment of desperate longing. The mother, again, searching for her young. Do we see **Figure** *screaming behind the mask?*

No nonsense now, get to the end:

Dennis   WHY DO YOU ALWAYS DISTURB ME WHEN I'M WATCHING ME SEXCAMS?!

Miriam   Don't shout at me like that, Dennis! If our son Johnny were still with us he wouldn't have it, Dennis! He wouldn't have this!

Dennis   Well, he's not with us is he! He's fucking DEAD. Jesus FUCKING Christ that FAG-music! TURN IT DOWN! TURN IT DOWN!

Beat.

She's been sitting on this for years:

Miriam   God forgive me. God forgive me for saying this but I wish it was you that had died and not our Johnny, Dennis . . . Oh god . . . I miss my Johnny . . .

Dennis   The only reason he killed himself –

Miriam   No, Dennis! Don't you dare! Not in this house –

Dennis   – the only reason he fucking killed himself –

Miriam   NO!

Dennis   – is because of YOU! YOU AND YOUR FUCKING DRINK!

Miriam   NO! No no no no. It's not true!

Mendacious Lecturer   Is it truly possible to buy a state of mind in Harrods? I know the question . . . I can see you all now. Looking at me. The question . . . Mouths agape with sweaty necks and bated breath . . . It's resting on your collective tongues, waiting, full of anticipation to leap into existence . . . You've got no IDEA . . . Let me tell you . . . How to deal with all this pain in life? A single day! A single day! I've got a joke for you. GET OUT! Go on, just say it! GET OUT! GET OUT! GET OUT!

Torycunt   JOIN IN WITH ME NOW!

(*Singing*)
    Rule, Britannia,
    Britannia rules the waves

Glaswegian Woman
    Britons never, never, never shall be slaves.

Grieving Widow
    Rule, Britannia,
    Britannia rules the waves
    Britons never, never, never shall be slaves.

She collapses.

More intense. The world is fucked, fractured, falling shards of broken mirror everywhere:

Love_Me   Why do you always film me when I'm waking up?! You're such a fucker! Haha, no you are! You're such a cunt! . . . Stop! Hahaha. No, I love you more! I love YOU more! No, no, no, I love you more . . . I do, I love you more!

Glaswegian Woman   I love you . . . I love you . . .

Mendacious Lecturer   Falling, falling, in and out of love –

Miriam   Do you love me, Dennis?

Dennis   No, I fucking HATE YOU.

Love_Me   I love you.

Mendacious Lecturer   Hindu or Buddhist . . . GET OUT!

The police officer is fucking **Glaswegian Woman**.

Glaswegian Woman   Please love me . . . Uhh . . . Uhh . . . Uhh . . . Uhh . . . Help me . . . HELP ME . . .

The Gentleman's Keeper *throws* **Clubrat** *out into the rain. Worlds are colliding.*

Clubrat   You don't have to kick me, you fucking BRUTE! Don't leave me out here . . . Please . . . You can't do this to me – I'm on the Spectrum!

Glaswegian Woman   'Scuse me, darling, I don't suppose you've got a couple of coins to get me on the bus?

Clubrat   Sorry love, it's not my problem . . .

The briefest passing moment of kindness:

Glaswegian Woman   I like your dress.

Clubrat   Thanks . . . It was my mum's. Fuck sake, here you go . . . it's not much.

Glaswegian Woman   Thank you, darling . . . Thank you . . . Thank you . . .

Descending back into cruelty:

You hurt me, Officer . . . You really hurt me . . . Please, Officer. My kids . . . I just want to end it . . . Please, Officer, do me a kindness . . . Please, Officer . . . Please . . . Kill me! KILL ME!

Mendacious Lecturer   Falling, falling, in and out of love –

Miriam   Love me, Dennis!

Dennis   Get out.

American Pornstar   Oh my god, it's in my pussy!

Mendacious Lecturer   . . . I'm drowning . . .

Glaswegian Woman   OFFICER!

Miriam   Love me!

Glaswegian Woman   PLEASE!

Dennis   GET OUT!

Miriam   Where will I go, Dennis?! It's three in the morning!

Dennis   GET OUT!

Miriam   Dennis, please don't do this to me . . . please . . .

Dennis   GET OUT!

Miriam   Calm down and eat your dinner, Dennis . . .

Dennis   These beans are fucking SOUR. THEY'RE SOUR! SOUR SOUR BEANS!

Beat.

Miriam   Well, they'll be your last.

Dennis (*spitting them out in disgust*)   What've you fucking done to them?!

Miriam   RAT POISON, DENNIS . . .

Dennis   You fucking PIG-BITCH!

Dennis *is having a massive heart attack.*

Miriam *watching him.*

Dennis   . . . . . .

Miriam *watching him.*

Dennis   . . .

Grieving Widow   I'm coming to you, Bernie, I'm coming!

Singing in full voice now. A beautiful swansong calling to the other side.

Glaswegian Woman   KILL KILL KILL KILL KILL KILL KILL KILL MEEEEEEEE!

Mendacious Lecturer   Now after long and rigorous consideration, I think it is quite safe to say, that THIS . . . THIS . . . THIS . . . THIS . . . THIS IS NOT CULTURALLY SIGNIFICANT.

Miriam *watching him.*

Dennis   . . .

Miriam *watching him.*

Dennis *dies.*

Beat.

Miriam (*singing*)
  Beans, beans, they're good for your heart
  The more you eat, the more you fart
  The more you fart, the better you feel
  So eat more beans Dennis, with every meal!

Figure *bursting out of a coma. Utterly distraught. Have they all left?*

Mendacious Lecturer   Good evening ladies and ge –

Ends.

Printed in the USA
CPSIA information can be obtained
at www.ICGtesting.com
LVHW012010041124
795688LV00046B/1504

9 781350 512672